A *New* Practical Guide for Taking Control of Your $pending

by
Mr. Penny Pin¢her

Cover Design & Illustrations
by Straw Berry

ALL RIGHTS RESERVED
COPYRIGHT © 2018

Table of Contents

Forward 5
Introduction 6
Intended Audience 9
How to Use This Booklet 9
Internet References and QR Codes 11
Preventative Principles 12
   First principle: 12
   Second Principle: 13
   Third Principle: 14
   Fourth Principle: 14
   Fifth Principle: 15
   Sixth Principle: 16
   Seventh Principle: 16
   Eighth Principle: 17
   Ninth Principle: 17
Curative Principles 18
   First Principle: 18
   Second Principle: 20
   Third Principle: 21
   Fourth Principle: 22
   Fifth Principle: 23
   Sixth Principle: 23
   Seventh Principle: 24
   Eight Principle: 24
   Ninth Principle: 24
Low Hanging Fruits 26
   First Principle: 26

Level 1 Couponing 26
Level 2 Couponing 27
Level 3 Couponing 27
Second Principle: 28
Third Principle: 29
Fourth Principle: 30
Fifth Principle: 30
Sixth Principle: 30
Seventh Principle: 31
Last Principle: 33

> "little by little, a little becomes **A LOT**"
>
> — TANZANIAN PROVERB

Forward

Have you ever been so overwhelmed by a problem that you just let it go until it snowballed into a disaster? When a problem gets out of control, even thinking about it can make you feel helpless. A huge problem in our society is personal debt. If getting out of debt was an easy task, millions would not be suffering from it. There are no magical solutions, but with patience and modified habits you can start whittling down your debt. If you feel overwhelmed by your financial situation, then this book might be for you.

Why am I writing this book? There are no gimmicks here and I don't have a product to sell you. But I have seen family, friends, and colleagues utterly throttled by debt. As soon as a house was nearly paid off, they went to get another house and a new loan to go with it. As soon as the family car was a couple of years old, they went to trade it in for a pittance and get a new one. They bought new cell phones for the family every few years, and with all the trimmings too! Not to mention huge grocery bills and waste from over-buying. In their lives I saw stress, divorce, and not enough money to even help their kids with college. However, there is a solution to this problem. With a little careful planning and patience, you can live a debt free life. Being debt free is utterly priceless. I'm going to give you all my strategies for financial success.

The greatest care has been taken to not overwhelm you. You no longer have to run from your problem! You can start reclaiming your life by paying off and saving money, step by step.

Introduction

First of all, let me confess at the outset that I got the idea for this booklet from my wife. She convinced me that there are many families and individuals out there who could benefit from my strategies. I hope what you are about to read will help you take back the control of your finances and reduce much of the unnecessary stress in your life.

I recognize that financial challenges may vary from family to family and from person to person, nevertheless the guidelines that I am going to talk about in this booklet should be applicable to most if not all financial situations.

This booklet is divided into three main sections, namely **preventative principles**, **curative principles** and what I called the '**low hanging fruits**'. The preventative principles are designed to inhibit individuals from falling into financial difficulties and the curative principles are designed to get someone out of any financial difficulty as quickly as possible. As for the low hanging fruits, it contains a few of the best practices that if followed can save you anywhere from a few hundred to few thousand dollars a year.

I know these principles work and our family financial situation is living proof. Here are some highlights:
1. We purchased our house with cash. We don't live in a mansion, but rather something that is comfortable and good enough for our family needs.
2. We purchased our cars with cash. We did not buy brand new cars. Instead, we opted for reliable good used vehicles.

3. We do not owe a penny to any credit card company, not even department stores.
4. We have two kids in college and we are able to pay whatever is not covered by their scholarships. They will graduate college debt free.
5. Last year when our first son needed a car for his co-op rotation, we bought his car with cash.
6. This year our second son will start his co-op rotation and his car is in the driveway (purchased outright) ready for his rotation next month.
7. By the way, I am an engineer and my wife is a stay at home mom. We do not have a lot more income than a usual middle class family. That is to say, you can do it too.

All of this wasn't accomplished without financial discipline. My kids did not have cell phone service until they started college. They have been able to make do with free cellular services such as Freedom Pop. My wife and youngest child do not have paid cell phone service either. We bought the devices at very reasonable prices (thanks to the website SlickDeals etc.) and they have been able to make do with a mix of free cellular service and wifi.

As for me, I still do not have any cell phone service. What this means is that within the last 10 years, we saved at least $10,000 by not adopting the latest and greatest from the cell phone industry. Secondly, we never had cable. I estimate our savings to be about $14,000 simply by staying away from cable. No, I am not expecting everyone to go as far as we have, but I think everyone can figure out for himself and herself ways to reduce recurring expenses such as phone or cable bills.

I like to ask the readers to give me feedback, be it positive or negative, so that I can continue to improve the work and share the success stories with the reader in subsequent editions to provide encouragement for others struggling with financial challenges.

Share your story:

Mr. Penny Pin¢her
mrpennypinchersaves@gmail.com
USA
2018

Intended Audience

If you fall into one of the following categories, this booklet is for you:
1. You are stressed out about your financial situation and have a hard time keeping up with bills.
2. You feel like you need to improve your spending habits in order to get out of debt.
3. You are a couple starting a family who wants to cultivate a stable financial position from the start.
4. You are a young college graduate who needs good financial acumen to pay off student loans quickly.

How to Use This Booklet

This booklet is not intended to be read from cover to cover and then forgotten about. Instead, here is a technique for you to get the most out of this book.
1. Read the book from beginning to end marking along the way the principles that you think apply to you or that you are interested in trying.

I	B	M	N/A
√			

2. If you find that a principle <u>**does not apply**</u> to you, then mark it as follows:

I	B	M	N/A
			✖

Once you are done with the book, you will have marked all the principles that are of interest to you.

3. The next step is to start to apply the principles one or two at a time. Whichever ones you decide to start practicing, mark them as follows indicating that you began the practice of that principle.

I	B	M	N/A
√	√		

4. If you find yourself applying a particular principle successfully over a period of time where you start to see tangible results consistently, you can acknowledge your mastery of the principle and mark it as follows indicating that this principle is now part and parcel of your financial discipline.

I	B	M	N/A
√	√	√	

5. Continue in this fashion until you have gone through all the principles that you marked during your first read-through. Don't forget to revisit the N/A's to see if they are still not applicable for your situation.

6. Last but not least, please do not forget to give us feedback as to what worked and what did not work for you so that we may continue to improve these principles and add new ones as necessary.

Internet References and QR Codes

I included several references from the internet. The full URL is given for each case in the footnote. Recognizing that typing the full link can be error-prone and frustrating, I am including a QR code for each link. All you have to do is to scan the image using a **free** QR code reader on your smart phone and it will take you to the site with one additional click.

Here is an example:

Preventative Principles

These are intended to reduce the chance of someone falling into debt.

First principle:

I	B	M	N/A	Make your purchases with cash and avoid credit card or debit card purchases to the greatest extent possible.

The reason for this is that when you make the purchase with cash you physically see the money disappearing from your wallet or purse right before your eyes and this will help you reduce spending. Whereas with credit card or debit card purchases, you don't feel anything and so you will continue swiping until the next credit card bill shows up - but it will be too late to do anything about it.

Someone might say that this will not work in this day and age because we buy a lot of merchandise online. I would respectfully disagree. In fact, when you make an online purchase, you can move an equivalent amount of cash from your wallet or purse to a different location so that you actually feel the spending personally. And when you are about to buy something online, you don't make the purchase unless you have enough cash in your wallet to cover it. I can guarantee that this method will help reduce spurious purchases.

In addition, if you stick to your cash purchase principle, it is unlikely that you will have enough cash on you at all times to buy everything you are tempted to buy. Furthermore, the urge to buy something is usually a temporary one and if you can avoid it by not having enough cash, you will likely lose the interest in the item later on.

Furthermore, if you cannot pay off all the balance on your credit card, then interest will start accumulating. Let's walk through a quick example from ReadyforZero[1].

"Let's say that you have $1,000 on your card, and the credit card calculates your minimum as 2.5% of your total balance, then your minimum payment is $25 every month. If your annual interest rate, or APR, is set at 18%, you owe $180/year on your $1000 balance in interest charges. You end up paying $300/year in minimum payments ($25/month times 12 months). So that's only $120 that you're actually paying off on the principal balance ($300 in minimum payments minus $180 you owe in interest). So your balance is still $880 after a year of you making monthly minimum payments. It will take you 5 years and 3 months to pay off the credit card, and you end up paying a total of $1,566, or $566 in interest charges."

What this means is that in fact you end up paying $1,566 for something that should have cost only $1000 had you used cash, check, or even debit.

Second Principle:

I	B	M	N/A	Avoid 'one-touch' or 'one-click' purchases like the plague.

The easier you can make a purchase the more likely you

---

[1] Taken from http://blog.readyforzero.com/pay-minimum-credit-card/

are going to do it. The one-click purchases online or certain ridiculously easy payment methods using your smart phone are not accidents but they are designed to make you spend money more easily. The convenience comes with a hidden risk and cost - you spend your money without feeling or noticing that you are spending it!

Third Principle:

I	B	M	N/A	
				When you are about to buy something using a credit card, if you do not have the cash in your checking account to pay the credit card off immediately, think ten times before making that purchase.

This will prevent you from spending money that you don't have. Some might argue that they will get paid in a few days and so they will be able to pay off the credit card bill. This may work for some, but in my experience, <u>people tend to overestimate how much they have and underestimate how much they owe</u>. The end result is that sooner or later they fall short and start paying interest and late fees to credit card companies.

Fourth Principle:

I	B	M	N/A	
				Before purchasing something just because it is dramatically discounted, ask yourself if you really need it.

The commercial industry is very sophisticated in that they sometimes employ specialists who insert subliminal messages in their ads which can lead consumers to buy things they do not need. You don't want to fall victim to sneaky commercials. You want to keep a statement running through your head while shopping, "I will only spend money on what

I really need not what the commercials suggest that I need."

Fifth Principle:

I	B	M	N/A	You need to reprogram your brain to process phrases such as "bundle and save" or "buy now and save more" in exactly the opposite way.

That is to say, you tell yourself: if I don't make this purchase, I will save X amount but if I do make it, I will spend all that money. Do I really have to make this purchase? When in doubt, step away and give yourself time to think about it. In most cases, you can always return and buy it later if you really want to.

Sixth Principle:

I	B	M	N/A	Do not renew your cell phone following the product cycle. Keep your old cell phone as long as possible.

One of the ways that wireless carriers trick consumers is that when you pay off your device they send a message that says, "You can get a new phone and your monthly bill will stay the same!" As soon as your old cellphone payment ends, they start you on a new one, so you don't feel that you are paying any more for it. If you choose not to upgrade, your monthly bill will go down and you can save the extra cash or use it to pay off other debt.

Seventh Principle:

I	B	M	N/A	Don't be lured by the deceivingly low monthly payments of a purchase.

In many instances, businesses get consumers to buy by emphasizing the monthly (or weekly) payment- not the total cost of the purchase. Make it a habit to quickly calculate how much you will end up paying in total instead of focusing on the monthly amount.

When you see the total cost and how many years you'll be paying for it, you will be more likely to look at other alternatives or to not even buy it -especially if it is an optional or luxury purchase.

Eighth Principle:

I	B	M	N/A	Many stores offer extended warranty at the time of the purchase of a product. You should decline it.

Don't buy extended warranties. It'd be better to set aside the money for potential repairs[2]. I personally opt out of every one of them. I don't recall regretting this decision except for one time with a dishwasher. It turns out that the particular model I bought was a complete lemon, but had I read the reviews prior to my purchase, I would not have bought it. It was a good reminder that even great companies sometimes make lemons. In any case, as long as one properly researches a product, you most probably don't need a protection plan.

Ninth Principle:

I	B	M	N/A	When looking at the prices, always round up.

Often we see prices like $89.95 or $13,999. What most people will maintain from these two prices are approximately $80 and $13,000. This is in fact exactly what the designers of the price tags want you to do. As a conscientious consumer, I suggest you round up so that you remember these two prices as $90.00 and $14,000. That way, you have a more accurate picture of how much you will end up paying if you decide to move forward with the transaction.

---

2   https://www.consumerreports.org/shopping/dont-buy-extended-warranties/

Curative Principles

These principles are intended to get someone out of debt. One of the basic facts you need to keep in mind while working on getting out of debt is that <u>minimum payments will keep you in debt</u>[3] while maximizing the interest earnings of the lenders.

First Principle:

I	B	M	N/A	Pay more than the minimum payment on your credit card bill.

Let's take the ReadyforZero example again:

"Let's say that you have $1,000 on your card, and the credit card calculates your minimum as 2.5% of your total balance, then your minimum payment is $25 every month. If your annual interest rate, or APR, is set at 18%, you owe $180/year on your $1000 balance in interest charges. You end up paying $300/year in minimum payments ($25/month times 12 months). So that's only $120 that you're actually paying off on the principal balance ($300 in minimum payments minus $180 you owe in interest). So your balance is still $880 after a year of you making monthly minimum payments."

Credit card companies do not calculate the minimum payment amount to help you pay off your balance faster. They're a business, and like any business, they want to maximize <u>their profits.</u> They do this through interest charges and hope

3   Taken from https://www.csmonitor.com/Business/Saving-Money/2016/0403/Four-reasons-you-should-pay-more-than-the-minimum-payment

that you will pay just the minimum payment because it maximizes their profits. The longer it takes you to pay off your credit card, the more total interest you pay on your principal balance. By only paying the minimum payment, you're only slowly paying off the principal balance that continues to sit there accruing more interest every month.

"Using the above example and the ReadyforZero credit card debt calculator, let's see how much MORE interest you're paying if you only pay the minimum payment of $25 month versus if you chose to pay $50/month.

If you pay the minimum, then it will take you 5 years and 3 months to pay off the credit card, and you end up paying a total of $1,566, or $566 in interest charges.

If you were to pay $50/month, then it will take you 2 years and one month to pay off the credit card, and you end up paying a total of $1,205, or $205 in interest charges.

While $25 more a month might feel like a stretch for your budget, think of the small ways you can save to put that extra $25 a month toward your credit card bill. By paying just $25 a month more on your credit card, you save yourself over $350 in interest charges and pay off your card twice as fast[4]."

"The common advice is never to carry a balance on a credit card and always pay off balances before their

---

4   Taken from http://blog.readyforzero.com/pay-mini-

due dates, completely avoiding minimum payments. If that's not possible, throw any mount more minimum toward your balance to chop it down faster[5]."

Second Principle:

I	B	M	N/A	Pay more than the monthly payment on your car loan.

When you only pay the minimum, you are paying so little toward the principal balance every month and you're actually increasing the amount of time you'll be in debt. This increases the time you'll keep making interest payments, which causes the total amount you're paying to grow.

Using a simple car loan calculator, just look at the difference in interest paid on a $25,000 car loan at 3% interest when the term is 60 months, compared to a 72-month loan[6]:

- 60-month loan: Payments are $449 per month and $26,953 total (or $1,953 more than the loan amount).
- 72-month loan: Payments are $380 per month and $27,349 total (or $2,349 more than the loan amount).

The situation is even worse if your interest rate is higher.
- 72-month loan: A $25,000 car loan at 6.49% interest results in payments of $420 per month for a 72 months,

---

mum-credit-card/

5   Taken from https://www.csmonitor.com/Business/Saving-Money/2016/0403/Four-reasons-you-should-pay-more-than-the-minimum-payment

6   Taken from https://www.csmonitor.com/Business/Saving-Money/2016/0403/Four-reasons-you-should-pay-more-than-the-minimum-payment

and a total of $30,249 paid (or $5,249 more than the loan amount).

Third Principle:

I	B	M	N/A	Pay more than the monthly payment on your mortgage.

The mortgage magic in prepaying your mortgage comes from paying down your outstanding loan balance with additional principal payments. Here is an example shows that if you pay an additional $100 a month on a 30 year $100,000 loan, you will end up paying your bank $156,028.95 instead of $182,406.71 reducing the total interest payment by $26,377.76[7] and pay off the mortgage 8.5 years earlier.

	New Mortgage	New mortgage with additional principal payments	Difference
Loan Amount	$100,000	$100,000	
Interest Rate	4.5%	4.5%	
Loan Term (months)	360	258	-102 (-8.5 years)
Loan Payment	$506.69	$506.69	
Additional Principal Payment	-	$100	
Total Monthly Payment	$506.69	$606.69	+$100
Total Interest Expense	$82,406.71	$56,028.95	-$26,377.76

---

7 Taken from https://www.bankrate.com/finance/mortgages/pay-extra-toward-mortgage-principal.aspx

Fourth Principle:

I	B	M	N/A	Try to do without unlimited data and minutes for your cell phone service.

Unless your business depends on your cell phone, you should minimize your cell phone and data usage where you can make do with the least expensive plan. If at all possible, look for free cell phone service providers such as FreedomPop. Sure, the coverage and quality may not be as good as the paid plan, but it's free. Reducing any recurring payments such as a phone bill is one of the most effective ways to trim your spending. Suppose you are on a payment plan for 24 months and paying $100 a month. If you can reduce your bill by half, in 24 months you will have saved $1200.

Fifth Principle:

I	B	M	N/A	Minimize your cable spending or eliminate it.

My family has never had cable. Assuming that the average cable bill is about $65, we have saved approximately $14,000 over eighteen years' time. If you have internet access, I would argue that you can easily do away with cable altogether[8]. I know that internet access is not dirt-cheap but it can replace your cable and home phone if you decide to use a VOIP (voice over IP) phone service such as Magic Jack and the like for $30-40 a year. In addition, the research that you would conduct on the internet and the subsequent savings plus savings from the coupons you can print out will pay for your internet in no time.

Sixth Principle:

I	B	M	N/A	Reduce your electricity bill.

I see some people who have outside lights burning day and night. For the life of me I can't fathom why they would waste money like that. If you feel like you need light outside your home, change the bulb to an LED and this will reduce your consumption. In any case make sure that the light is off during daylight hours and turn any lights off when you leave a room. You can also change the bulbs inside your house to LEDs. This will cause a noticeable reduction in your electricity bill. You may not think that a bulb or two is a big deal but it adds up over time. After 100% conversion to LEDs,

---

[8] A colleague told me that by switching to the Google TV, he is saving $55 a month. Another colleague said they eliminated cable alltogether saving $135 a month.

we were able to reduce our electricity bill by more than $50. That is at least $600 per year. Your savings will depend on the size of your home, your current lights and usage habits.

Seventh Principle:

I	B	M	N/A	Reduce your heating and air conditioning bill.

If you can reduce the set temperature of your thermostat one degree less than your desired temperature by wearing warmer clothes in winter, you will see a noticeable reduction in your bill. In the same way, if you can withstand one degree higher than your desired temperature in summer, you should also see the effect in your bill. In the meantime, make sure that you change the filters in accordance with the manufacturer's recommendations so that you don't reduce the efficiency of your heating/cooling system.

Eight Principle:

I	B	M	N/A	Reduce your water bill.

As you are using water, pay attention and ask yourself if you can reduce the amount of water used and still accomplish the objective; be it washing the dishes or watering the plants or taking a shower.

Ninth Principle:

I	B	M	N/A	Select a compact vehicle for your commute to work if you can.

In the following table I have calculated approximately, what the gas cost will be for three different commuting distances of 15, 25 and 35 miles for 5 years. I also included three vehicle choices which have gas mileage anywhere from 16 to 35mpg. Depending on the vehicle choice and commute distance you can spend[9] anywhere from $3,829 to $8,395 less if you use a compact economy car instead of a large SUV. This does not take into account the differences in maintenance costs between the vehicles.

Distance to work (miles)	Travel per Year (miles)	Gas Spending for Five Years			SUV-Compact
		SUV (16mpg)	Mid-size (23mpg)	Compact (35mpg)	
15	7920	$7,054	$4,907	$3,225	$3,829
25	13200	$11,756	$8,178	$5,374	$6,382
35	18480	$16,459	$11,450	$7,524	$8,395

---

[9] I used $2.85 as the price per gallon in my calculations.

Low Hanging Fruits

First Principle:

Level	I	B	M	N/A
1				
2				
3				

Couponing is one of the best ways to save money, especially for weekly grocery shopping.

It takes time and experience to take full advantage of couponing. That is why I divided it into three levels. As you master one level, you can move to the next one.

Level 1 Couponing

Before you set out to buy something, be it in a department or hardware store or even online, do a quick Google search on the internet to see if there are any coupons available. You will be surprised how much you can save with coupons like 10, 20 or 30% off.

Level 2 Couponing

In addition to level 1 couponing, use a price matching strategy. Before you checkout, see how much the same product is selling for online. Many stores will match the price of big online retailers.

At the very least, download Ibotta. When you get the hang of Ibotta, you can try checkout 51 and maybe even SavingStar. Take your time so that you won't feel overwhelmed. Don't listen to those coupon stories about how they got $900 worth of stuff for $10! Your journey will not be the same as anyone else's. Sometimes different cities have better deals than others. Don't sweat it! Getting overwhelmed can be your worst enemy. Start small, get to know the coupon rules and how to deal with cashiers. Little by little, your $5 savings will turn into $20 and that will turn into $50 and it will go on and on.

Level 3 Couponing

When you are feeling a little more adventurous, here are a few more sites for you to explore:

1. couponcabin.com
2. retailmenot.com
3. thekrazycouponlady.com
4. southernsavers.com (Even if you live in the North)
5. northerncheapskate.com (Even if you live in the South)
6. totallytarget.com
7. thecouponingcouple.com (Target ads are put up early.)
8. iheartcvs.com (CVS ads are available about a week early!)
9. iheartwags.com
10. coupons.com
11. ibotta.com

Many sites have great communities that will patiently help you better understand how to coupon. If you feel a bit overwhelmed, simply begin by buying a Sunday paper and clipping the coupons you think you might use.

A few tips you won't get anywhere else: First of all, don't get mad at the cashiers if they can't accept your coupon. I have heard cashiers at a big box store talk about how another co-worker got fired for accidentally taking a coupon she wasn't supposed to. Take any big issues up with management or call customer service. Pay attention to which cashiers understand how coupons work. You will find that some cashiers are very astute and others are clueless. Save time and get in the line of the expert who doesn't have to keep calling a manager over to explain things.

Second Principle:

I	B	M	N/A

Do not trade in your car!

Did you know that car dealers are making more money from used cars than new ones? They pay very little for trade-ins and turn around and sell them for an arm and a leg. Depending on the state of your vehicle, you are almost guaranteed to be able to sell it on craigslist, cars.com or autotrader.com and get anywhere from one thousand to several thousand dollars more than what the dealer would pay you. It only takes a little bit of time and patience. Be careful though. Do not accept personal checks from individuals and do your transactions at a bank using a cashier's check or cash.

Third Principle:

I	B	M	N/A	Should you buy a used car from a dealer? Yes, but keep the following in mind.

Car dealers are thought by some to be the greediest people on the face of the earth. That is why I do not recommend buying a used car from a dealer except if you follow the procedure that I am about to reveal:

1. Look at the used car inventory of the dealerships online.
2. If you find a car that you like, look for the CARFAX link. Most dealers, especially the big ones, provide a free CARFAX report. Click on the link and go all the way to the end of the records and look for last entry along the lines of "**Dealer Inventory Vehicle offered for sale**". If the car was offered for sale more than two months ago by the dealer, it must have gone through several price reductions already and the dealer is ready to negotiate with you especially if you can pay in cash[10]. What happens is that if the large dealers keep a car too long on their lot, it counts against them and thus they have every incentive to sell it even if they don't make a lot of money on it. If they cannot sell it, they will have to send it to an auction[11] and they know

---

10   We bought three cars like this from big name dealers after having noticed that the cars had been on their lots more than two months. We bought one of the cars and used it for about a year and a half putting about 12,000 miles on it. We later sold it on craigslist for the same price that we bought it for after having fixed the front shocks for a few hundred dollars.

11   Sometimes, they send it to a different dealership owned by the same parent company. You should be able to figure out if this is the case.

full well that other dealers will not pay anywhere near what an individual will pay.

Fourth Principle:

I	B	M	N/A	
				Avoid using vending machines.

Bring your own soda or snacks to work instead of buying them from vending machines. I have seen people paying up to $1.50 for a can of soda when in fact they can buy it for as low as 19¢ a can at the store with coupons. The same is true for snacks. Don't look down on a daily saving of $1.31. If you drink a soda everyday, we are talking about saving $250 a year.

Fifth Principle:

I	B	M	N/A	
				Avoid eating out regularly.

Cheap fast-food is bad for you health and healthy good food in a restaurant is bad for your budget. The healthy and inexpensive alternative is to cook and eat at home.

Sixth Principle:

I	B	M	N/A	
				Try to do some vehicle maintenance yourself.

Do as much of the vehicle maintenance as you feel comfortable after taking ALL the precautionary measures recommended by the car manufacturer and the tools you are using. For example, my kids and I now have three German cars. If we changed the oil at the dealership, it would have cost us $600 for all three cars every few months. But since we are DIY people, it costs $50 a car or $150 for all three using full synthetic oil and a German-made oil filter.

We have saved several thousand dollars over the last few years by replacing the brakes, starter, VENOS cellonoids, thermostat, window regulators and valve cover gaskets ourselves. I am not suggesting that everyone should be able to do full maintenance of his or her vehicle. I am just saying that you should figure out your capabilities and limits to see if there is anything you can do to save money as far as vehicle maintenance is concerned.

Seventh Principle:

I	B	M	N/A	Try to do some home maintenance and needed improvement yourself.

Several years ago when we bought our house, my son and I changed the locks on the doors and that was the full extent to which I had done any home maintenance in my whole life.

After moving in, I started calling around and getting quotes from at least three contractors at a time for various tasks that we needed done around the house. I found out that more often than not the prices were way out of our budget. Not only they were quoting ridiculous numbers for labor but I even caught one guy citing material costs that were 200%-300% more than what was available in the hardware store.

We decided to do the work ourselves. Today, we have a brand new kitchen, brand new bathroom, crown molding all around the house, wainscoting in the hallway and certain rooms, a carport converted to a two-car garage, and we painted the full house and replaced all the doors. In the process, we have saved about $30,000 and increased the value of the house by about 50%.

Once again, not everyone has the means or the time to do all of this but you are the best judge of what you can and cannot do. My suggestion is this- take your time and do your research before venturing into any home improvements. Read several blogs (My wife's hands down favorite DIY blog is: www.addicted2decorating.com) and watch multiple DIY videos to make sure that you are fully comfortable with what you are about to do. No two houses are identical and you never know what you are going to find behind those walls.

Last Principle:

I	B	M	N/A	
				Don't be penny-wise and pound-foolish!

So far we have been talking about saving, saving, and saving. I don't want you, the reader, to lose sight of the global picture where you are concerned with sparing every penny but ignore the larger picture and end up spending more. Always keep in mind the global picture and the consequences of your choices.

A New Practical Guide for Taking Control of Your $pending

ready?

A New Practical Guide for Taking Control of Your $pending

www.ingramcontent.com/pod-product-compliance
Lightning Source LLC
Chambersburg PA
CBHW031514210526
45464CB00007B/2914